Effective Communication Skills

Instructor's Guide
Second Edition

Marsha Ludden

Effective Communication Skills Instructor's Guide, *Second Edition*

© 2002 by JIST Publishing, Inc.

Published by JIST Works, an imprint of JIST Publishing, Inc.
8902 Otis Avenue
Indianapolis, IN 46216-1033

Phone: 1-800-648-JIST
E-mail: info@jist.com

Fax: 1-800-JIST-FAX
Web site: www.jist.com

Note to instructors. This book was designed to be used with the *Effective Communication Skills* workbook. The books are also supported by a related video. Call 1-800-648-JIST or visit www.jist.com for details.

About career materials published by JIST. Our materials encourage people to be self-directed and to take control of their destinies. We work hard to provide excellent content, solid advice, and techniques that get results. If you have questions about this book or other JIST products, call 1-800-648-JIST or visit www.jist.com.

Quantity discounts are available for JIST products. Call 1-800-648-JIST or visit www.jist.com for a free catalog and for more information.

Visit www.jist.com. Find out about our products, get free book chapters, order a catalog, and link to other career-related sites. You can also learn more about JIST authors and JIST training available to professionals.

Acquisitions Editor: Lori Cates Hand
Development Editor: Mary Ellen Stephenson
Cover Designer: Aleata Howard
Page Layout Coordinator: Carolyn J. Newland
Proofreaders: Jeanne Clark, Veda Dickerson

Printed in the United States of America

06 05 04 03 02 01   9 8 7 6 5 4 3 2 1

We have been careful to provide accurate information throughout this book, but it is possible that errors and omissions have been introduced. Please consider this in making any career plans or other important decisions. Trust your own judgment above all else and in all things.

ISBN 1-56370-853-1

About This Book

The *Effective Communication Skills Instructor's Guide* is much more than just an answer key for the exercises in the *Effective Communication Skills* student workbook. It also contains

- "Additional Activities" to expand each chapter's lessons and to provide students with a variety of classroom interaction.
- Worksheets that you can photocopy and distribute to students for self-directed practice.
- Topics for students to reflect on in their communications journals.
- "For Your Information" sections that cite chapter-related Web sites, books, and other up-to-date teaching resources.

You can use all of these activities and resources in the *Instructor's Guide* to help you tailor your communication classes to fit your time frame and meet your students' needs and interests. The workbook and *Instructor's Guide* make up a very flexible and adaptable curriculum.

This *Instructor's Guide* is intended to be both a time and energy saver for you. It provides material not found in the student workbook, *Effective Communication Skills*. You may use these suggestions to expand classroom activities and reinforce student learning as needed.

In this book you will find

- Chapter Purpose—A brief review of the information covered in each chapter of *Effective Communication Skills.*
- For Your Information—Web sites, books, and other materials that may be helpful to you as outside resources.
- Additional Activities—Ways to meet students' needs and interests through creative classroom activities.
- Suggested Journal Assignments—Ideas that relate to topics in the chapter and help students practice written communication skills.
- Worksheets—Self-directed activities that may be copied for use by students.
- Answer Keys—Answers to "Check It Out" and "Check Your Vocabulary" activities.

About *Effective Communication Skills*

Effective Communication Skills introduces students to the many ways that people interact with each other. It may be used to

- Make students aware of the importance of communication in both work and social situations
- Help students understand that communicating is done with both words and wordless messages
- Help students develop this valuable life skill by practicing in an informal group situation

Effective Communication Skills has been written to encourage your students to use communication skills in the classroom as well as in their daily lives. Reading the text is important. Encourage your students to read it. Use it as the basis for group discussion. Strive to provide time for student participation throughout the course.

You will find exercises called "Check It Out" in each chapter, and the answer keys are in this *Instructor's Guide*. These activities require your students to both read and write. Some of these exercises require only a one- or two-word answer. Others need to be answered in sentence form. In some cases, the students will use their personal experiences to answer questions.

At the end of each chapter, an exercise called "Check Your Vocabulary" reviews key terms introduced in the reading. You may use this exercise to help a student who did not fully understand any part of the chapter.

Introduction

Preparing to Teach

Begin your preparation by reading *Effective Communication Skills*, as well as this *Instructor's Guide*, and doing each exercise from the student's viewpoint. Some of the answers are very distinctly correct. Others will involve students' opinions or life experiences. Your willingness to share your personal experiences will set an example for your students.

Because *Effective Communication Skills* provides numerous opportunities for discussion, you may want to write some notes in the margins of your book. One of your students may share an experience that you may want to use in a future class.

Plan a basic schedule for class time. This will allow the class to run smoothly and keep on task. It will help in scheduling audio-visual equipment, special guests, field trips, and other extras. If the schedule is interrupted, do not panic. You can revise the schedule and continue from that point.

Prepare your teaching materials. You may have some handouts that you will be distributing in the classroom. Check this *Instructor's Guide* for additional exercises and worksheets that you can use with your class. If you expect your students to do work outside of class time, you may prepare that information. Schedule guests, videos, field trips, and any other extra elements that you want to use.

Check out the classroom. The classroom temperature is important. It is difficult to concentrate when you are too hot or too cold. Learn where the thermostat is located in the classroom. Find out how and if you can adjust it.

Lighting is important. Know where the electric switches and outlets are located. If lights are not working, tell someone who is responsible for maintenance. Make sure that no one is facing a window that lets the sun glare into his eyes.

Think about the room arrangement. Be sure that students sit where they can see any visual you are using. Find a space where you feel comfortable. The classroom should focus on this area. You should be able to face the entire class and not have your back to anyone.

Think about how you want the desks or tables and chairs arranged. If you plan to use small groups, consider how easily furniture can be moved to form these groups.

Listen to the noise level. If possible, avoid noise and interruptions. Keep the classroom as quiet and free of interruptions as possible.

Set Class Expectations

You need to communicate what you expect of the students. Decide what you will require from each one. Write out these specific requirements and prepare a copy for everyone. Some instructors have students sign this contract on the first class day and keep it on file.

You need to tell students what you expect concerning attendance. This may already be set by the institution, but students may need a reminder. If class begins at a particular time, state what that time is. Define what "being late to class" means. If being "in class" means being seated quietly, say so.

List the materials (book, pencils, pens, paper, and so on) that should be brought to each class meeting. Be specific about due dates for work done outside the classroom.

Set standards for conduct in the classroom. Students should be respectful in their treatment of themselves, fellow students, and you, the instructor.

Set the Mood

You are the most important element in the class. Your attitude is contagious. Be enthusiastic. Be flexible. Listen to your students to learn their needs.

Be positive. Point out the strengths of individuals and the whole group. Be generous with sincere praise. Use criticism only if it cannot be avoided. If you need to criticize someone, find a way to do it privately. As you communicate, you are the key to the success of this learning experience.

The First Class Meeting

A brief introduction of yourself is an excellent way to begin the first class session. Sharing the following information will help you develop a positive relationship with your students. The introduction could include

- Your name
- Facts about your personal or family life
- Interests or hobbies you have
- Something about your educational background
- Some humorous or relevant event involving you and your communications with others

Since you will be encouraging your students to participate and communicate throughout this course, set an example from the first moment of the class.

Introduce the Course

A brief description of the purpose and procedures for the course will help the students understand your expectations. Talk about rules. Be specific. Be clear in explaining what you expect students to do and how they will be held accountable for these responsibilities.

Make sure that each person has a copy of *Effective Communication Skills*. Read the title of the book. Have students brainstorm words that come to mind when they think of *communication.* List the words on an overhead or chalkboard.

Read the introduction of *Effective Communication Skills* together. Discuss the different ways of communicating presented in the introduction. Check the list that the class made. Circle any words that appear both in the introduction and the list. Add any ways that are not already on the list.

Discuss the fact that communication is both sending and receiving messages. In order to communicate effectively, an individual must have the skills to do both.

Additional Activity: Getting to Know Each Other

This activity will allow students to get to know each other in a small group. It will help them feel more comfortable in sharing with the whole group later.

Divide the class into groups of four or five people. Ask the members of each group to introduce themselves, using the following information as it is appropriate for your class:

- Name
- Personal or family life
- Special interests/hobbies/sports
- Reason for taking this course
- What you expect to learn in this course

List these topics on an overhead or a board for students to see during this activity. Encourage students to ask questions within their groups.

Additional Activity: The Art of Effective Communication Video

A video, *The Art of Effective Communication,* is available from JIST. For information about this video, go to the JIST Web site: www.jist.com.

Additional Activity: Journalizing

You may want your class to keep a communications journal throughout the class, or you may use this activity as a one-time assignment. Keeping a journal throughout the course will give your class an opportunity to improve written communication skills.

Each entry should be three to four paragraphs, but never more than a page. You may want to assign a topic that relates to the communication skill being presented at that time. If you do not want to assign a topic, encourage students to write about a topic of their choosing to just express their thoughts. Since journals are personal, no one should be expected to share journal entries with the entire class.

Suggested Journal Assignments

Two or more ideas for class-related journal assignments are suggested in various chapters of the *Instructor's Guide.* You may choose a journal assignment question from these suggestions or list all the suggestions and let each individual choose what he or she would like to write about.

To introduce journalizing in your first class, ask the students to write three or four paragraphs dealing with the following questions. It is not necessary to answer every question. The questions may also be used to get students to think about their personal communication skills.

- Think of someone you find easy to talk with. Why is talking to this person easy?
- When do you find it most difficult to talk to another person? Why?
- How do you communicate at school? Whom do you communicate with? How have your communication skills affected your learning?
- Do you have a job? How do you communicate on the job? Whom do you communicate with?

What Is Communication?

Chapter Purpose

Chapter 1 of *Effective Communication Skills* presents different types of communication including verbal and nonverbal interaction. Students will become aware of problems that can develop when effective communication does not take place, especially in work situations. The workbook provides opportunities for students to understand how their personal communication skills have been affected by outside influences.

For Your Information

For more information about skills that employers are seeking in employees, see the government report on the 21st Century Workforce Initiative at the Web site

http://www.dol.gov/dol/21cw

Additional Activity: It Takes Two

This activity shows that communication involves two people sharing thoughts.

Ask two students to come to the front of the classroom. Have the students sit in two chairs that are back to back. Give student #1 a pencil and drawing paper. Give student #2 a simple drawing of a house. Student #1 should not see the drawing.

Using only words, student #2 must try to describe the drawing to student #1. Student #2 may not use specific terms telling what the picture shows, such as "house," "window," "door," "chimney," or "smoke." Instead, words such as "square," "rectangle," "triangle," and "wiggly line" may be used. Student #1 may not ask any questions while attempting to duplicate the drawing. The two must remain back to back the entire time. You may want to set a timer to add more pressure to the situation (3–4 minutes). When time has run out, keep the drawing.

Again have two students come to the front. This time the students may face each other.

Student #1 should have a pencil and drawing paper. Student #2 should be given a simple picture of a train engine. Student #2 may not use the word "train," "wheel," "cow catcher," "smokestack," or "engine." Terms such as "triangle," "rectangle," "circle," and "square" may be used.

This time, student #1 may ask questions, although he cannot look at the drawing. Student #2 may point and look at student #1's drawing as he gives instructions. Allow three to four minutes to complete the drawing. At the end of the time limit, display both drawings.

Compare the two drawings. Encourage the participants to express their opinions of how they felt in both situations. Discuss how using gestures, having eye contact, and having the give-and-take of both participants made it easier to do the drawing.

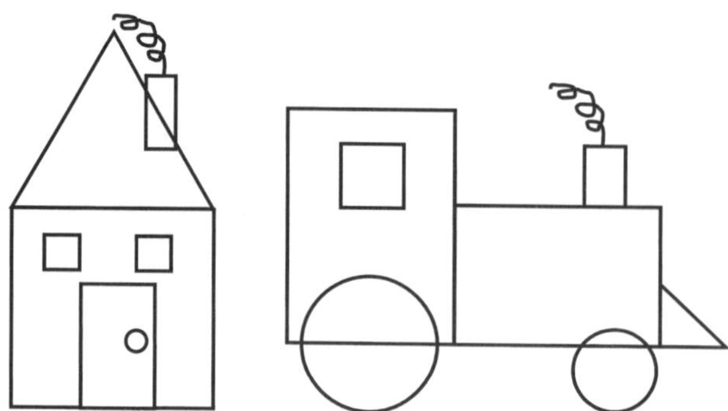

Using the same simple shapes—rectangles, circles, triangles, and wiggly lines—two artists might draw very different pictures, depending on the type of communication taking place. As the exercise shows, communication involving questions, answers, and gestures makes following directions much easier. Two-way communication means two people are participating in the same conversation.

Additional Activity: Communication Skills Needed on the Job

Use this activity to make students aware of the importance employers place on good communication skills.

Have students bring in or provide copies of employment help wanted ads from the newspaper. Instruct students to go through the ads to find different jobs that require communication skills. Students may highlight the ads and share them with the class during discussion.

Suggested Journal Assignment

Ask your students to write three or four paragraphs dealing with the different ways they communicate. It is not necessary to answer every question.

- What do you think is your strongest communication skill? Why?
- What do you think is your weakest communication skill? Why?
- What communication skill would you most like to improve? Why?

Chapter 1 Answer Key

Check It Out 1-1

The answers will vary depending on each individual's interpretation of the situation. Several possible answers are given on the next page.

Situation No. 1

1. *What message is Tasha sending Nick?*

    I am angry.

    The meeting is none of your business.

    I don't want to talk about it.

    I don't want to answer any questions.

    I just want to be alone.

2. *What message is Nick sending Tasha?*

    I am happy to see you.

    I am interested in what happened at the meeting.

    I want to talk to you.

Situation No. 2

3. *What message is Tasha sending Nick?*

    I am thirsty.

    I am glad to see you.

    I am happy.

    If you aren't going to talk to me, I'll just leave.

4. *What message is Nick sending Tasha?*

    I don't want to talk to you.

    This magazine is really interesting.

    I would just like to read without being bothered.

    I want to be left alone.

Check It Out 1-2

1. verbal	9. receiving
2. conversation	10. evaluate
3. negative	11. self-confidence
4. millions	12. unacceptable
5. nonverbal	13. employees
6. communication	14. job
7. impress	15. speak
8. sending	

Check It Out 1-3

The answers to this exercise will vary depending on each individual's choices.

List three examples of verbal communication:

Possible answers: Conversation, speeches, radio, television, plays, movies, videos, vocal music, classroom teaching.

List three situations where listening skills are needed:

Possible answers: Taking telephone messages, getting directions, learning in a class, following instructions, understanding what a customer is telling you.

List three examples of nonverbal communication:

Possible answers: Reading, writing, e-mail, body language, eye contact, hand gestures.

List three examples of written communication:

Possible answers: Newspapers, magazines, books, letters, notes, memos, e-mail, signs, brochures.

List three ways of communicating using technological means:

Possible answers: Telephone, voice mail, e-mail, computer, fax machines, videos.

Check It Out 1-4

Answers will vary depending on each individual's personal experiences.

Check It Out 1-5

When discussing this exercise, encourage students to give an example of how the worker might use a particular skill and why it would be important in the workplace. Students might list skills in addition to those mentioned here, depending on their interpretation of each worker's responsibilities.

Workplace No. 1

Uses proper English.	Uses the telephone properly.
Uses appropriate body language.	Expresses ideas clearly.
Writes legibly.	Takes accurate messages.
Listens to others.	Understands nonverbal communication.
Speaks clearly.	Listens to instructions.

Workplace No. 2

Uses proper English.	Uses the telephone properly.
Uses appropriate body language.	Expresses ideas clearly.
Writes legibly.	Takes accurate messages.
Listens to others.	Understands nonverbal communication.
Speaks clearly.	Listens to instructions.

Workplace No. 3

Uses proper English.	Speaks clearly.
Writes legibly.	Expresses ideas clearly.
Listens to others.	Listens to instructions.

Workplace No. 4

Listens to others.	Expresses ideas clearly.
Speaks clearly.	Listens to instructions.

Check Your Vocabulary

1. D: communication skills
2. G: written communication
3. A: communication
4. I: technological communication
5. L: slang
6. F: verbal communication
7. H: listening
8. B: speaker
9. E: nonverbal communication
10. J: interpret
11. K: reading
12. C: listener
13. M: secret language
14. O: colloquialisms
15. N: e-mail

Worksheet: Communication in Your Daily Life

This activity helps students realize the different ways they have interchange with others each day. Use it as an outside assignment. Students may share their information during class discussion. Keep a simple tabulation of each type of communication used. The class can observe what types of communication are used more often.

Run off the form on the following page. Instruct the students to use the worksheet to make a list of different people they meet during the day. Under Person, they may describe the person; for example, "man on the street corner," "older brother," or "parking lot attendant." For Type of Communication, they should select an answer from the list at the top of the worksheet.

Communication in Your Daily Life

Directions: Each day you have contact with many people. Some are friends and family. Some are part of your work or school experiences. Others are strangers. No matter how you meet these people, you will communicate with them in some way.

Write a description of six people you meet today. Look at the types of communication listed below. Find at least one way that you communicated with each person.

Nonverbal communication

Written communication

Verbal communication

Listening

Technological communication

Person	**Type of Communication**
1. ____________________________	____________________________
2. ____________________________	____________________________
3. ____________________________	____________________________
4. ____________________________	____________________________
5. ____________________________	____________________________
6. ____________________________	____________________________

Effective Listening Skills

Chapter Purpose

Chapter 2 of *Effective Communication Skills* presents the importance of listening in the communication process. Students will become aware that listening involves more than just hearing words. Listening is a choice. They can be either passive or active listeners. Listening for a particular reason means paying attention to key words and evaluating nonverbal clues that the speaker uses.

For Your Information

For more information on listening skills and hearing, go to these Web sites:

http://www.nidcd.nih.gov—National Institute on Deafness and Other Communication Disorders

http://www.indiana.edu/~eric_rec/—ERIC Clearinghouse on Reading, English, and Communication

Check the library for books and other information about listening and hearing. Two books that may be helpful are *Listening: The Forgotten Skill (Self-Teaching Guide)* by Madelyn Burley-Allen and *The Good Listener* by James E. Sullivan.

Additional Activity: What Is Listening?

Have two students role-play the conversation between Millie and John in the section "What Is Listening?" in *Effective Communication Skills.* Discuss the difference between hearing and listening.

Additional Activity: Barriers to Listening

People create barriers to listening by their own choices. Have the class brainstorm a list of actions that interfere with listening.

Read each of the following situations in class. Decide what barrier is hindering effective listening.

Alternative Suggestion: Divide the class into small groups. Give each group a situation. Have students role-play these barriers. After each role-play, have the class point out the barrier to listening.

Situation No. 1: Interrupting—Rhonda, Shaun, and Colin are talking about last night's concert. Jolene joins the group and immediately starts talking about her new job without letting anyone else talk.

Situation No. 2: Faking It—Jason is describing the problems he had with the auto shop that just worked on his car. Bryan sits staring off into space, nodding his head, and mumbling "Yeah!" occasionally. Jason finishes his story and asks, "So, what should I do?" Bryan suddenly looks at Jason with a shocked look on his face.

Situation No. 3: Poor Eye Contact—Heather is explaining the latest product line to Anthony just before he leaves work for the day. Anthony keeps looking at his watch and staring at the clock at the store entrance.

Situation No. 4: Thinking About What You Will Say—Terri is telling Jenny about her vacation in Mexico last month. While Terri is talking, Jenny is thinking, "Wait till she hears about my trip to Brazil last winter. She is really going to be impressed."

Situation No. 5: Daydreaming—Mr. Jameson is giving directions for the term paper due in two weeks. Jasmine is sitting at her desk, staring out the window and twisting her hair.

Situation No. 6: Not Asking Questions—Lance's supervisor has told him to get the monkey wrenches from the storeroom and set up a special sale display. Lance is not sure what type of wrenches he is looking for. He goes to the storeroom and looks for them. After a half hour, he still hasn't started setting up the display.

Additional Activity: Focused Listening

Explain to the students that they are going to do a listening experiment. For the next three minutes, no one is to talk. Each student will list on paper everything he hears during this time. Set a timer for three minutes.

At the end of the three minutes, compile a group list on an overhead or chalkboard. Next, have the group point out those sounds that they heard before the silence.

Talk about how our minds can block out distractions when we are listening. We choose to listen.

Suggested Journal Assignment

Ask your students to write three or four paragraphs dealing with the following questions. It is not necessary to answer every question.

- Do you recall a time when you heard but did not listen? What happened because you did not listen?

- Do you recall a time when you chose not to listen? Why did you choose to not listen?

Chapter 2 Answer Key

Check It Out 2-1

After students have completed the Listening I.Q. in this Check It Out, display the following chart to let them rate themselves as listeners.

Total Points	Listening I.Q.
9–10	You're a great listener.
7–8	You have room to improve.
0–6	Hello, in there! You're not listening!

Check It Out 2-2

Conversation No. 1

Rochelle is a passive listener. She makes no comment about the situation. She leaves the decision to Jolene.

Conversation No. 2

Henry is an active listener. He listens to the instructions and asks a question when he doesn't have all the information he wants.

Conversation No. 3

Carmen and Lamont are passive listeners. They hear Mr. Sargent, but they are not listening. They are active listeners to their own private conversation.

Conversation No. 4

Anthony is an active listener. He stops what he is doing and asks Tina to repeat what has happened to her.

Check It Out 2-3

The answers will vary depending on the location of each classroom.

Check It Out 2-4

The answers will vary. Here is a possible way to answer. The key words are in **bold** type.

Step 1: **First**, get out a toothbrush and toothpaste.

Step 2: **Next**, put toothpaste on the toothbrush.

Step 3: **Now**, wet the toothbrush. **First**, brush the teeth at the back of your mouth.

Step 4: Reach to the back of the teeth and brush. **Finally**, brush your tongue.

Step 5: **Last of all**, rinse your mouth with water. Clean your toothbrush.

Check It Out 2-5

The answers to this exercise will vary depending on the radio and television commercials that students listen to.

Check Your Vocabulary

1. C: hearing impairment
2. E: active listening
3. G: evaluate
4. I: directional words
5. A: hearing
6. J: landmarks
7. D: passive listening
8. F: key words
9. B: listening
10. H: sequence words
11. K: distance words

Worksheet: Listening Facts

This activity can reinforce information about listening found in Chapter 2 of *Effective Communication Skills*. It may be used as an outside assignment.

Run off the form on the following page. Tell the students that each sentence is false. On the line below each sentence, they are to change it to a true statement. You may use the following statement as an example for the class.

Passive listeners look at the speaker and respond to her words.

Corrected statement: **Active** listeners look at the speaker and respond to her words.

Worksheet Answer Key

Note: Students may phrase their sentences differently. Answers should be similar to the following.

1. An active listener listens while the speaker is talking.
2. Hearing is an involuntary physical activity.
3. A good listener asks questions.
4. Thinking about what to say next will harm your listening skills.
5. An active listener does not finish the speaker's sentences.
6. Nonverbal communication is needed to evaluate a speaker's message.
7. A hearing disability will affect listening.
8. Listening and hearing are not the same.
9. Interrupting a speaker demonstrates poor listening skills.
10. Looking at a speaker is important to listening effectively.

Listening Facts

Directions: Read these false statements about listening. Rewrite each sentence to make it a true statement.

1. An active listener talks while the speaker is talking.

   Corrected statement: ____

   ____

2. Listening is an involuntary physical activity.

   Corrected statement: ____

   ____

3. A good listener never asks questions.

   Corrected statement: ____

   ____

4. Thinking about what to say next will improve your listening skills.

   Corrected statement: ____

   ____

5. An active listener finishes the speaker's sentences.

   Corrected statement: ____

   ____

6. Nonverbal communication is not needed to evaluate a speaker's message.

   Corrected statement: ____

   ____

7. A hearing disability will not affect listening.

   Corrected statement: ____

   ____

8. Listening and hearing are the same.

   Corrected statement: ____

   ____

9. Interrupting a speaker demonstrates good listening skills.

   Corrected statement: ____

   ____

10. Looking at a speaker is not important to listening effectively.

    Corrected statement: ____

    ____

Oral Communication

Chapter Purpose

Chapter 3 of *Effective Communication Skills* shows the significance of oral communication in daily life. Students will become conscious of their speaking mannerisms and grammar. They will learn ways to converse with others in social and business situations. Speaking before groups is also discussed.

For Your Information

For more information on speech and language, go to these Web sites:

http://www.nidcd.nih.gov—National Institute on Deafness and Other Communication Disorders

http://www.professional.asha.org—American Speech-Language-Hearing Association

Additional Activity: Starting a Conversation (Follow Up to Check It Out 3-4)

Have students look at the conversation topics they listed in Check It Out 3-4. Ask students to choose one of the topics and write five questions that could be used to start a conversation using that topic. Point out that they need to write open-ended questions.

Additional Activity: Group Introductions

Give your students an opportunity to speak informally to the class. Try to keep this very low key. For many people, speaking to a group is upsetting.

Divide the class into groups of two. Have the students interview each other using the following questions.

- What is your name? What is your nickname?

- Where do you live? How long have you lived there? What do you like or dislike about your home?

- Do you work? How long have you worked there? What do you like about your work?

- What do you like to do in your spare time?

After they interview each other, give the students time to put together an introduction of the other person. Have the students come back into the group with the partners sitting together. Have each student introduce her partner to the class.

Additional Activity: Grammar Rating Scale (Use with Check It Out 3-2)

Use the following scale to rate students in grammar usage.

Correct Answers	Score
19–20	Excellent
14–18	Need to review
0–13	Weak area; need to improve

Suggested Journal Assignment

Ask your students to write three or four paragraphs dealing with the following questions. It is not necessary to answer every question.

- Do you recall a conversation when you had to tell someone you did not agree with him? Describe the situation. How did you tell him? How would you change the way you told him?

- Do you recall a time when you did not feel comfortable speaking to a group? Describe it. What would you do to feel better when speaking to a group?

Chapter 3 Answer Key

Check It Out 3-1

1. mumbling
2. speech pattern
3. tongue
4. monotone
5. speech therapist
6. oral communication
7. low voice
8. tool
9. habits
10. definitions
11. jumbled
12. grammar
13. articulation
14. whining

Check It Out 3-2

1.	Let	11.	set
2.	aren't	12.	any
3.	sings	13.	Learn
4.	were	14.	written
5.	may	15.	lay
6.	swum	16.	don't
7.	ate	17.	frozen
8.	sings	18.	were
9.	threw	19.	Bring
10.	said	20.	come

Check It Out 3-3

The answers will vary. Some suggested answers are included here.

Situation No. 1

Closed question: Have you ever been to Washington?

Open-ended question: What have you enjoyed most about the trip?

Situation No. 2

Closed question: Do you like volleyball?

Open-ended question: How did you learn to play volleyball so well?

Situation No. 3

Closed question: How many pizzas did we deliver tonight?

Open-ended question: Why do you think we were so busy tonight?

Situation No. 4

Closed question: How long have you lived in this neighborhood?

Open-ended question: What do you like most about living in this neighborhood?

Check It Out 3-4

Answers will vary depending on the person the student chooses.

Check It Out 3-5

The sequence words are **first** and **Next**. Readers might also draw time sequence clues from the words **After, When, finally,** and **The rest**. The written descriptions will vary.

Check It Out 3-6

The clue words are **First, Second,** and **Third**. The written conversations about asking for a raise will vary.

Check It Out 3-7

The clue words are **First, Step two, Step three, Step four,** and **Last**. The instructions for making a sandwich will vary.

Check It Out 3-8

The compliment is "**You make the best breakfast in the world.**" The conversations about not joining the team will vary.

Check Your Vocabulary

1. E: mumbling
2. B: definition
3. K: exaggeration
4. A: oral communication
5. I: open-ended question
6. L: time sequence
7. F: speech pattern
8. C: grammar
9. J: malicious gossip
10. D: speech therapy
11. H: closed question
12. N: assertive approach
13. G: intrapersonal speech
14. M: logical approach
15. O: interpersonal speech

Worksheet: Listening to Your Voice

The aim of this activity is to give students an opportunity to listen to their own voices. If these questions are not appropriate for your class, you may use other questions or use a reading.

Students will need audio recorders and tapes for this activity. Give each student a copy of the Listening to Your Voice worksheet found at the end of this chapter.

Worksheet: Speaking Correctly

This activity reinforces using correct language in daily life. It may be used as an outside assignment.

Give each student a copy of the Speaking Correctly worksheet found at the end of this chapter. Tell the students that each sentence is written using careless grammar and slang terms. On the line below each sentence, students are to rewrite the sentence using appropriate English.

You may use the following statement as an example for the class.

I ain't goin' to the partee, no way man.

Corrected sentence: I am not going to the party.

Worksheet Answer Key

Note: Students may phrase their sentences differently. Answers should be similar to the following:

1. Please bring that tool to me.

2. Please be quiet. I can't hear the radio.

3. Franco doesn't have any lunch money.

4. I could go to the movie with you.

5. Let Josie borrow your CD.

6. I'll be with you shortly.

7. Yes, sir, how may I help you?

8. The Moores were helping with the dinner.

9. I don't know how your window was broken.

10. I am sorry. We are out of that shampoo.

Listening to Your Voice

Directions: How does your voice sound? With a partner, record the following interview. Have your partner read the questions. Answer each question in complete sentences. Do not write anything. Just answer the questions as your partner asks them. When you finish, trade jobs with your partner and record the conversation a second time.

Question 1: What is your name?

Question 2: If you were allowed to decorate and furnish your own apartment in any way you wanted, how would you do it? What furniture and other items would you place in your apartment? Where would you place these items? How would you decorate the apartment?

Question 3: If you were given a million dollars to be spent on any special project, what project would you choose? You can't spend the money on yourself. Give at least three reasons for your choice.

Question 4: If you could take a month's vacation to any location, where would you go? Give at least three reasons for your choice.

With your partner, listen to the recordings. Listen to yourself carefully. How does your voice sound? Do you hear any irritating qualities? How clear are the words you speak?

Do you speak too quickly? Do you speak too slowly? Do you repeat phrases or clear your throat? How difficult is it to speak and think about your answer at the same time? Is your answer logical? Does it make sense?

To improve your voice, you must be conscious of your voice. You need to listen to yourself as you speak. Recording yourself is an excellent way to hear yourself. After listening to yourself, you need to evaluate any weaknesses. With conscious effort, you will improve your speaking ability.

Speaking Correctly

Directions: The following sentences use careless grammar and slang terms. Read each sentence. Rewrite each sentence using correct grammar and appropriate words.

1. Hey, you, take that tool to me.

   Corrected sentence: ____

2. Shut up! I can't hear the radio.

   Corrected sentence: ____

3. Franco ain't got no lunch money.

   Corrected sentence: ____

4. You know, I could, you know. go to the movie with you.

   Corrected sentence: ____

5. Leave Josie borrow your CD.

   Corrected sentence: ____

6. Don't sweat it! I'll be with ya in a split second.

   Corrected sentence: ____

7. Yeah man, what can I do for youse?

   Corrected sentence: ____

8. The Moores was helpin with the dinner.

   Corrected sentence: ____

9. I don't have no idea how your window got busted.

   Corrected sentence: ____

10. Sorry lady. We is all outa that kinda shampoo.

    Corrected sentence: ____

Communicating Over the Telephone

Chapter Purpose

Chapter 4 of *Effective Communication Skills* will help students understand how to use the telephone properly. The differences between talking on the telephone and having a face-to-face conversation are discussed. Students will have the opportunity to learn about the information available in a telephone directory through several hands-on activities. They will learn about making different types of telephone calls and how to handle problems that might arise with telephone use. They will practice leaving and taking telephone messages.

For Your Information

For more information about using the telephone, go to the Web site of the telephone company in your area. Check the library for books and other information about telephone use and courtesy. One book that may be helpful is *Telephone Skills from A to Z* by Nancy Friedman.

Additional Activity: The Importance of the Telephone

Talk about the importance of the telephone in our lives.

Make a list of the ways businesses use telephones. How do businesses depend on the telephones?

Make a list of the ways the telephone is used in our personal lives. How have the students used the telephone in their personal lives?

What happens when the telephone system goes out for even one day?

Additional Activity: Your Personal Telephone Voice

This activity introduces students to the idea that a telephone voice is different from the voice used when talking to a friend face-to-face. You may use this discussion as an introduction to the worksheet activity Rating Your Personal Telephone Voice.

Talk about the differences between face-to-face and telephone conversations. Point out that during a telephone conversation

- Nonverbal communication means nothing because the speakers can't see each other.

- The speaking voice and the words spoken are more important because the conversation is totally verbal.

Background noises are more distracting because the telephone magnifies sounds, making it difficult to hear clearly.

Talk about the need to use your voice to show the caller that you are interested in the conversation. Discuss how to show interest by developing your own telephone voice. Work together to create a list of ways to develop a good telephone voice. These may include the following:

- Speak clearly. Don't mumble.

- Pronounce words precisely.

- Speak into the telephone receiver.

- Don't eat, drink, or chew when using the telephone.

- Use the right voice volume—not too loud or too soft.

- Speak at the right speed—not too fast or too slow.

- Avoid using a monotone voice. Raise and lower your voice as you talk.

- Think about the person on the other end of the telephone line. Remember that you are talking to a person, not to this machine called a telephone.

Additional Activity: Discussing Telephone Courtesy

Use this activity to help students understand that a business telephone conversation requires some organization and courtesy to impress the caller. Discuss the following points about a business telephone.

- Know how you are to answer the telephone. Often this is the name of the business and perhaps your name. For example, say, "Hello, this is Howe's Office Supply. This is Kerry."

- If you are already talking on the telephone and must answer a second line, politely ask the first caller to hold and briefly answer the second call. For example, say to the second caller, "Hello, this is Howe's Office Supply. Please hold." Then complete the first call.

- Be friendly. Deal with the purpose of the call. For example, ask, "How may I help you?"

- Use polite words. For example, say, "May I have your telephone number, please?"

- Be professional. Use businesslike language. Don't be too casual. For example, say, "Mr. Minor will be in the office this afternoon. May I have him call you?"

- If you answer a telephone call for another person, be careful about the information you give the caller. For example, your supervisor may not want everyone to know that she is home this week recovering from an operation. For example, say, "Miss Apple is out of the office this week. May I take a message?"

- Write down the message and include your name. Then the person receiving the message will know who to talk to if the message is not clear. Politely ask the caller to repeat the message if there is something you don't understand. For example, say, "Please repeat your telephone number."

- End the call when the caller indicates that he is done. Always thank the caller for calling. For example, say, "Mr. Daniels, thank you for calling. I will make sure that Miss Fry gets this news today."

- Be careful when hanging up. Don't slam the receiver into the cradle.

The worksheet Telephone Courtesy is available at the end of this chapter.

Suggested Journal Assignment

Ask your students to write three or four paragraphs dealing with the following questions. It is not necessary to answer every question.

- How have you personally used the telephone this week? How have you used it socially? How have you used it for personal business?

- How have you used the telephone at work this week? How else do you use it in the workplace? How does knowing how to use the telephone correctly help you on the job?

Chapter 4 Answer Key

Check It Out 4-1

1. receiver	7. end
2. voice	8. Smiling
3. clearly	9. talk
4. slower	10. drinking
5. gently	11. radio
6. identify	12. excitement

Check It Out 4-2

These answers would be checked in the checklist.

1. Yellow Pages	11. Business White Pages
2. Yellow Pages	12. Residence White Pages
3. Residence White Pages	13. Yellow Pages
4. Business White Pages	14. Government White Pages
5. Government White Pages	15. Yellow Pages
6. Yellow Pages	16. Yellow Pages
7. Yellow Pages	17. Business White Pages
8. Yellow Pages	18. Yellow Pages
9. Government White Pages	19. Government White Pages
10. Business White Pages	20. Business White Pages

Check It Out 4-3

1. 911

2. Answers will vary. Look under Telephone Services.

3. Call directory assistance.

4. This number varies from state to state. There may also be a local number to call.

5. Answers will vary. Look in the yellow pages under Hospitals.

6. Call the customer service number. Follow the instructions you are given at this number.

7. Answers will vary. Look under Non-Emergency Assistance. Students need to understand that 911 is NOT the number to call in this non-emergency situation.

8. Call directory assistance.

9. Answers will vary. Look in the yellow pages.

10. Answers will vary. Look under Non-Emergency Assistance. Students need to understand that 911 is NOT the number to call in this non-emergency situation.

11. Answers will vary. Look in the yellow pages under Social Service Organizations.

12. Ask Gina for her telephone number.

13. Answers will vary. Look under Telephone Provider Information in the residence white pages.

14. Look in the government white pages under United States Postal Service.

15. Look in the government white pages.

Check It Out 4-4

1. To give the person time to get to the telephone.

2. Hang up. Call back later.

3. Use your first and last name to let the person know exactly who is calling.

4. The dial tone lets you know that the telephone is ready for use. When you don't get a dial tone, hang up and try again.

5. Thank the person for their time or simply say "Good-bye."

6. Check the telephone directory.

7. Your name, telephone number, and a brief message telling the reason for the call.

Check It Out 4-5

1. Dial 1-986-744-3321.

2. Look up Santa Fe area code in the telephone directory. Dial 1-505-610-8213.

3. Dial 0-405-153-2302. Wait. Listen for tone. Dial calling card number 207-262-8041-2637.

4. Dial 1-800-587-2302.

5. "Is this 606-4488?" If the answer is "No," say, "I'm sorry. I have dialed the wrong number." If the answer is "Yes," ask, "Is this Ed's Coffee Shop?" If the answer is "No," say, "I must have the wrong number." Hang up and check the number before you try again.

6. Dial 1-897-8934.

7. Dial 0-478-333-9216. Wait for the operator. Tell the operator you are making a collect call. Give your name.

8. Dial 0-765-297-4433. Wait for the operator. Tell the operator you are placing a person-to-person call to Hal Hansen.

9. Dial 10-10-2020. Wait for tone. Dial 1-343-903-5758.

10. Call the customer service number listed in the telephone directory. Ask that these numbers be blocked.

Check It Out 4-6

Conversation No. 1

> To: Jonathon Phillips
> Time: 9:30 a.m.
> Date: April 4, Monday
> Caller: Yvonne Garcia
> Telephone Number: 663-5112
> Message: Represents the Windows on the World Book Program. Wants to set appointment.
> Signed: *Student's signature*

Conversation No. 2

> To: Marilee Wendall
> Time: 11:15 a.m.
> Date: July 11, Tuesday
> Caller: Malcolm Collins
> Telephone Number: 893-4536
> Message: Wants hair styled tomorrow morning.
> Signed: *Student's signature*

Conversation No. 3

> To: Mr. Williams
> Time: 1:00 p.m.
> Date: June 12, Friday
> Caller: Bob Carter
> Telephone Number: 742-0033
> Message: Can't play golf this afternoon. Maybe tomorrow. Return call.
> Signed: *Student's signature*

Conversation No. 4

> To: Karen Monroe
> Time: 2:30 p.m.
> Date: March 12, Thursday
> Caller: Deborah Friar
> Telephone Number: 337-8469, work phone
> Message: Wants a parent conference. May call her at work from 7 to 3.
> Signed: *Student's signature*

Check Your Vocabulary

1. R: area code	13. A: receiver
2. M: direct dialing	14. E: white pages
3. G: voice mail	15. Q: busy signal
4. L: calling-card call	16. T: collect call
5. B: cell phone	17. F: yellow pages
6. O: directory assistance	18. K: long-distance call
7. N: 911	19. I: unlisted telephone number
8. D: telephone directory	20. S: person-to-person call
9. J: operator-assisted call	21. U: wrong number
10. P: dial tone	22. W: telemarketing
11. V: toll-free numbers	23. X: harassing call
12. H: prepaid calling card	24. C: cradle

Worksheet: Rating Your Personal Telephone Voice

All the students should have a copy of the telephone conversation found at the end of this chapter.

Each student will read the conversation as if he were talking to Mr. Randall on the telephone. You may use a telephone to make the experience more realistic. Each student will be evaluated by the other students using the following categories:

1. Clear speech

2. Volume (loud/soft)

3. Rate of speech (fast/slow)

Use a point system (1-5) to rate each student in each category—5 meaning very good; 4, good; 3, average; 2, poor; 1, needs improvement.

Alternative Suggestion: Select three to five students to act as the panel of judges. Each judge will need a set of index cards with the numbers 1 to 5. The judges can rate the students by holding up the cards and using the same categories as above.

Worksheet: Telephone Courtesy

This worksheet, Telephone Courtesy, could be used as a review of the lessons offered in Additional Activity: Discussing Telephone Courtesy. Students will need to apply what was discussed. They will read the first statement and reword it in a more businesslike way. This worksheet is available at the end of this chapter.

Worksheet Answer Key

Note: Students may phrase their sentences differently. Answers should be similar to the following:

1. "Mr. Linder is not in the office. May I take a message?"
2. "Hello, this is Marsha. Who is calling, please?"
3. "Ms. Walden is out of the office this week. May I take a message?"
4. "I am sorry. I can't hear you. Could you speak louder?"
5. "Mr. Riggs is out of the office today. He will be back tomorrow. May I take your name and telephone number?"
6. "Please repeat the telephone number."
7. "She is not at her desk. May I give her a message?"
8. "Hello, could you please hold? I will be with you soon."
9. "Thank you for calling. Good-bye."
10. "Mr. Sapp is gone for the day. May I take a message?"

Rating Your Personal Telephone Voice

Directions: Read the following conversation aloud so others can evaluate your telephone voice.

"Hello, Mr. Randall. This is Lynn Robbins from Gordan's Auto Repair. I am calling to tell you that your car is ready to be picked up. We will be open till 7 this evening. Our service manager will be on duty till then, if you have any questions."

Rate each caller using the following scale:

5	Very good
4	Good
3	Average
2	Poor
1	Needs improvement

Student	Clear Speech	Volume (Loud/Soft)	Rate of Speech (Fast/Slow)

Telephone Courtesy

Directions: The sentences in this exercise are not courteous or businesslike. Read each sentence and reword it. Write a sentence that would be useful and appropriate in a business situation.

1. "Mr. Linder has disappeared. Hang on! I'll go track him down."

   Reworded statement: ____

   ____

2. "Hi, there! Who is this?"

   Reworded statement: ____

   ____

3. "Ms. Walden is having her wisdom teeth removed today. She will be back next week."

   Reworded statement: ____

   ____

4. "Look, buddy, you need to speak up. I can't hear you."

   Reworded statement: ____

   ____

5. "Mr. Riggs is out of the office today. Let me give you his home telephone number."

   Reworded statement: ____

   ____

6. "Hey! Slow down. I didn't get that telephone number."

   Reworded statement: ____

   ____

7. "She can't talk right now. She's in the ladies' room."

   Reworded statement: ____

   ____

8. "Hold on. Be with you in a minute. I'm on the other line."

   Reworded statement: ____

   ____

9. "Okay! Bye!"

   Reworded statement: ____

   ____

10. "Mr. Sapp is gone for the day."

    Reworded statement: ____

    ____

Messages Without Words

Chapter Purpose

Chapter 5 of *Effective Communication Skills* will help students realize that messages are being sent to others even when no words are spoken. The eyes, the hands, and the face are all means of sending messages without using words. Others interpret these nonverbal actions to determine what is being communicated. Students will learn to think about what messages they are sending and how to interpret nonverbal messages.

For Your Information

For more information about nonverbal communication, check the local library for recent books and other information. These books may be helpful: *Nonverbal Communication in Human Interaction* by Mark L. Knapp and *Gestures: The Do's and Taboos of Body Language Around the World* by Roger E. Axtell.

For information about American Sign Language, go to the Web site

http://www.aslta.org—American Sign Language Teachers Association

Additional Activity: Guest

Contact a person who has studied sign language to share this knowledge with the class.

The guest may share about training for sign language as well as demonstrate signing to the group. Encourage the students to observe all of the signer's actions. Help them understand that signing is more than just using the hands to speak. Facial expressions and eye contact are also important.

Additional Activity: A Picture Tells a Story

Ask students to choose an emotion, such as happiness, sadness, or thoughtfulness. Using magazines, newspapers, and other sources of pictures, have each student create a collage showing that emotion. Have the students share the completed works and guess the emotion that is depicted in each case.

Additional Activity: Body Posture

Use this activity to help students understand how body posture affects the way we respond to each other.

Ask two people to pretend to be students in a classroom. Privately give instructions to the actors. Ask one to use good body posture as he enters and sits in the classroom. Ask the other to slouch as she enters and sits in the classroom. Select a third student to be the teacher. Explain that only the teacher may speak during the activity.

The two students should enter the room and take seats in front of the group. The student acting as teacher will give them instructions for completing a paper.

After the role-playing is finished, discuss what happened. What reaction did the teacher have to the slouching student? What reaction did the teacher have to the other student? What impression does good posture give? How does poor posture affect other people's attitudes toward you?

Alternative Suggestion: Have the actors portray two individuals going for a job interview instead of students. Have the actors convey good and poor eye contact, rather than posture.

Additional Activity: Silent Movie

Show a video without the sound. Have students write the nonverbal communication they observe and how they interpret the messages. Share their findings.

Additional Activity: An Experiment

Challenge your students to try an experiment. Ask them to smile at some strangers as they go about their daily activities. Have them record the situation and the reaction of the strangers. Share their experiences with the class.

Alternative Suggestion: Extend the experiment by having students avoid eye contact or frown at others. Share the results.

Additional Activity: Sit on Them

Each student will need a partner for this exercise. Partners should sit in chairs facing each other. The first student should sit on his hands. Without using his hands, he must tell his partner how to get from the room to the nearest exit.

It is now the second person's turn. Without using any hand movement, she must describe how to get to the nearest telephone from this room.

Have the group come back together. Discuss how individuals felt when they could not use hand gestures. Did the listener clearly understand the directions?

Suggested Journal Assignment

Ask your students to write three or four paragraphs dealing with the following questions. It is not necessary to answer every question.

- Think about your childhood. Do you recall any type of nonverbal communication that went on in your family? What was the message that you received when this nonverbal communication went on? Do you recall any nonverbal communication that was considered unacceptable by your family or friends as you were growing up?

- Think about different cultures. What nonverbal communication might be acceptable in one culture but not in another? What type of problems might develop in such a situation? How could such a situation be avoided?

- Give students a picture of an individual showing a particular feeling. Ask the students to write about that emotion and what might have happened to cause the emotion.

Chapter 5 Answer Key

Check It Out 5-1

Situation No. 1

1. *List the nonverbal actions Joanne uses to communicate to her customer.*

   Joanne grabs the credit card from the customer. She uses more force than needed to pass the card through the machine. She tosses the customer's purchases into the cart. She taps her fingers while waiting for the customer to sign the credit slip.

2. *What is Joanne's communication telling her customer?*

   Joanne is unhappy. She does not want to help this customer. She wants to leave work. She thinks the customer should have shopped earlier.

Situation No. 2

1. *List the nonverbal actions Joanne uses to communicate with her customer.*

   Joanne looks at her customers. She smiles. She whistles. She bags the purchases and hands them to the customer. She greets the other customers.

2. *What is Joanne's communication telling her customer?*

   Joanne is happy. She wants to make the customer feel important. She is helpful. She treats all her customers this way.

Check It Out 5-2

Possibility No. 1

Observe Glenda. Does she do this often? Ask others if they have noticed her doing this. Talk to Glenda if this irritates you. Ignore it if you are not bothered by it.

Possibility No. 2

Check outside. Is the wind blowing? Ignore it. The wind will stop blowing soon.

Possibility No. 3

Observe Glenda. Does she appear angry? Ask her if she is upset. Talk to her. Listen to her reason for her anger. Ignore her anger.

Check It Out 5-3

Note: Different answers may be used for each of these body actions. Below are some suggested answers.

1. The football player is happily excited. The player is taunting the other team.

2. The driver is challenging the other driver to react. The driver is angry with the other driver.

3. The player is frustrated. The player is thrilled at a great play.

4. The president wants everyone quiet. The president wants the meeting to begin.

5. The secretary is busy and acted without thinking. The secretary is angry.

6. The father is showing love. The father is greeting the child.

7. The mechanic is frustrated while working on the car. The mechanic is angry.

8. The student is stressed. The student is frustrated.

9. The officer is directing traffic. The officer is stopping traffic for an emergency.

10. The man is offering comfort. The friend is offering congratulations.

Check It Out 5-4

G   F   E

I   B   D

H   A   C

Check It Out 5-5

Skepticism

Calmness

Surprise

Happiness

Anger

Disappointment

Check Your Vocabulary

1. C: hand gestures
2. E: body posture
3. F: eye contact
4. G: personal space
5. D: facial expressions
6. B: body language
7. H: body action
8. A: nonverbal communication

Worksheet: Messages Without Words

This activity can be used as a review of nonverbal communication. It may be used as an outside assignment.

Worksheet Answer Key

1. hand gestures
2. agreement
3. Vulgar
4. eye contact
5. personal space
6. raised eyebrow
7. facial expressions
8. boring
9. observe
10. Body posture
11. cultures
12. formal
13. convincing
14. equal
15. overusing

Messages Without Words

Directions: Fill in the blanks using the following word bank.

personal space	formal
eye contact	boring
observe	vulgar
facial expressions	equal
agreement	body posture
raised eyebrow	cultures
hand gestures	overusing
convincing	

1. Pointing and waving are types of ______________ ____________________ commonly used by people.

2. Nodding the head is a body gesture showing ____________________ with the speaker.

3. ____________________ and threatening gestures are unacceptable in a social or business situation.

4. No __________ ________________ causes a speaker to believe that the listener is not interested in the conversation.

5. The imaginary area of privacy surrounding each person's body is known as ________________ ____________________.

6. A __________ ________ is a facial expression showing disapproval.

7. Emotions shown through the use of the mouth, the eyes, and head movement are called ____________________ ____________________.

8. A speaker, observing a listener staring out the window, might conclude that his topic is ________________.

9. To interpret nonverbal communication, you need to ____________________ the nonverbal communication and listen to the spoken communication.

10. __________ ____________ is the way a speaker's body is placed in relationship to the listener.

11. An act of nonverbal communication may not mean the same thing in two different ________________.

12. When the speaker sits behind a desk, the meeting seems more ____________________.

13. Crossed arms may indicate that a person is listening but needs more ________________.

14. When two people sit beside each other, communication is on an ________________ basis.

15. A speaker needs to avoid ________________ hand gestures.

Written Communication

Chapter Purpose

Chapter 6 of *Effective Communication Skills* introduces students to the need for written communication in both social and business dealings. They will discover different ways to write letters. Students will learn the correct form to use when writing letters. Knowing when to use the telephone and when to use written communication will be discussed.

For Your Information

For more information about letter writing, check the local library for books and recent information. Two books that may be helpful are *How to Say It: Choice Words, Phrases, Sentences, and Paragraphs for Every Situation* by Rosalie Maggio and *Effective Letters for Every Occasion* by Casey Fitts Hawley.

Additional Activity: Letter to the Editor

Together with the class, read some letters to the editor from newspapers. Discuss these letters. Who wrote the letter? What was the writer's purpose in writing the letter? Did the writer make his message clear?

As an outside assignment, have each person bring to class a list of issues that are currently important in the community. Newspapers and news programs are good sources of this information. Talking to others is another way.

In class, compile a group list of different issues. Have each person choose a topic from this list and write a letter to the editor concerning this issue. Collect these letters for later use.

Additional Activity: Letter of Appreciation

Ask your students to think of people who have helped them in their lives. Ask the students to write letters to these people thanking them for their kindness. Save the letters for later use.

Suggested Journal Assignment

Ask your students to write three or four paragraphs dealing with the following questions. It is not necessary to answer every question.

- Think about mail you receive. What type of written communication do you receive? How is this type of communication useful to you? How is it useful in handling your personal business?

- What type of personal communication do you receive that is social? How is written communication helpful in your social life?

- Have you ever seen any letters that have been saved by your family? Describe these letters. Why were they written? Who wrote them? To whom were they written? When were they written?

Chapter 6 Answer Key

Check It Out 6-1

This exercise involves writing a personal letter. The way it is done will vary with each student. The letter should include a heading, salutation or greeting, body, closing, and signature. The student should label these parts in the completed letter.

Check It Out 6-2

This exercise involves writing a thank-you note. The way it is done will vary with each student. The thank-you note should include a heading, salutation or greeting, body, closing, and signature. The student should label these parts in the completed letter.

Check It Out 6-3

Students will use the sample invitation in the text to answer the following questions.

Who is in charge of the event? The Computer Users' Group
What? Meeting
When? Thursday, May 23, from 7:30–9:00 p.m.
Where? Basement of Community Hall
Why? Guest speaker talking about computers and printers

Check It Out 6-4

Students will use the sample invitation in the text to answer the following questions.

Who is extending the invitation? Jenny Miller
What? Retirement Party
When? January 28, Noon
Where? Old Stone House Restaurant, 1455 Stony Road
Why? To honor Pauline Woods

Check It Out 6-5

The invitations in this exercise will vary with each student. Students should be able to answer these questions—who is giving the invitation, what is the event, when will the event take place, where will the event take place, and why is the event being held—for their own invitations.

Check It Out 6-6

This exercise involves writing a letter of request. Each letter will vary. Students should include and label the parts of the business letter: heading, inside address, salutation, body, closing, and signature.

Check It Out 6-7

This exercise involves writing a letter requesting a job application. Each letter will vary. Students should include and label the parts of the business letter: heading, inside address, salutation, body, closing, and signature.

Check It Out 6-8

This exercise is writing a consumer letter. Each letter will vary. Students should include and label the parts of the business letter: heading, inside address, salutation, body, closing, and signature.

Check Your Vocabulary

1. L: R.S.V.P.
2. A: personal letter
3. F: body
4. I: thank-you note
5. H: signature
6. K: invitation
7. B: heading
8. C: business letter
9. J: bread-and-butter note
10. G: closing
11. M: block form
12. E: salutation
13. O: letter of request
14. Q: letter of job application
15. N: modified block form
16. D: inside address
17. P: letter of consumer complaint

Worksheet: Word Usage

Use this worksheet to help people understand that using the right word is important in writing. It may be used as an outside assignment.

Worksheet Answer Key

Merilee hurried **to** the mailbox. Opening the box, she discovered a letter. Her eyes caught **sight** of the return address. "Oh!" she sighed. "**It's** from Henri. I haven't talked to him for a **week**."

Merilee hurried down the **road** to the house. Inside the house, she **read** the letter. How she wished Henri could be **here** with her. After reading the letter the **fourth** time, Merilee knew she could not **waste** another moment. She went **straight** to the telephone and called Henri.

"Darling!" she said. "Of **course**, I will marry you. Just send the **fare**, and I will **buy** our **plane** tickets to the **isles**."

Word Usage

Directions: Read the following story. Complete the story by circling the correct word from the pairs of words in parentheses. Although the words are pronounced the same, they do not have the same meaning. Choose the word that has the correct meaning in each sentence.

Merilee hurried (to, too) the mailbox. Opening the box, she discovered a letter. Her eyes caught (site, sight) of the return address. "Oh!" she sighed. "(Its, It's) from Henri. I haven't talked to him for a (weak, week)."

Merilee hurried down the (road, rode) to the house. Inside the house, she (red, read) the letter. How she wished Henri could be (hear, here) with her. After reading the letter the (forth, fourth) time, Merilee knew she could not (waist, waste) another moment. She went (straight, strait) to the telephone and called Henri.

"Darling!" she said. "Of (coarse, course), I will marry you. Just send the (fair, fare), and I will (buy, bye) our (plain, plane) tickets to the (aisles, isles)."

Getting a Letter to Its Destination

Chapter Purpose

Chapter 7 of *Effective Communication Skills* shows the correct way to address an envelope for mailing. Students will learn about the computerized method by which the United States Postal Service handles large amounts of mail on a daily basis. For faster and more accurate delivery, mail should be addressed in ways that help computerized postal machines read, code, and sort it.

For Your Information

For more information about mail and the United States Postal Service, go to this site:

http://www.usps.com—United States Postal Service

You can also contact the Postal Service's National Customer Support Center at (800) 238-3150.

Additional Activity: Addressing Envelopes

If you did the Additional Activity: Letter to the Editor in chapter 6, have each student address and mail his letter. Watch the newspaper. Someone may get published.

If you did the Additional Activity: Letter of Appreciation in chapter 6, have each student address and mail her letter.

Additional Activity: A Visit

Check with your local postal service. It may be possible to arrange a tour of the postal service facilities.

Additional Activity: Pamphlets

Several pamphlets written by the United States Postal Service are available through its Web site or at the Customer Support Center (800) 238-3150. Check it for information for your students.

Chapter 7 Answer Key

Check It Out 7-1

1. The print is too light.

2. The address is not all capital letters.

3. The print is too stylized.

4. The print is touching.

5. The entire address is not seen.

6. A design has been placed below the address.

7. The address is not straight.

8. Punctuation has been used in the address. The attention line has been placed below the address.

Check It Out 7-2

1. *Return Address:*
   Student's address
   Destination Address:
   MRS CHAR HAWTHORNE
   WALL REALTY
   869 E SILVER ST
   TOPEKA KS 66603-1234

2. *Return Address:*
   JOAN SMYTHE
   22 EVERGREEN VLY APT 7B
   WALDEN VT 05869-5678
   Destination Address:
   CECIL TURNOVER
   789 SPRING RD
   SUNSET TX 76270-8901

3. *Return Address:*
   Student's address
   Destination Address:
   GEORGE WASHINGTON
   PRES OF THE US
   1776 CHERRY LN
   MT VERNON VA 22121-3456

4. *Return Address:*
   BETSY FRAZIER
   RR 4
   SNOWBALL AR 72676-5432
   Destination Address:
   NEAL MADISON
   3400 S MERRILL DR
   HIGHLAND MN 55411-2332

5. *Return Address:*
   Student's address
   Destination Address:
   ATTN HEAD RANGER
   YELLOWTAIL STATE PARK
   PO BOX 451
   YELLOWTAIL MT 59035-5678

6. *Return Address:*
   JAMES ROBERTS
   5400 NORMAL BLVD
   PARKER GA 30316-4321
   Destination Address:
   DR KELLY FULLER
   CEDARVILLE HOSP
   7812 N MEDICAL PLZ STE 327
   CEDARVILLE OH 45314-3456

Check It Out 7-3

Students may practice folding a letter as illustrated in the exercise.

Check Your Vocabulary

1. K: postal clerk
2. L: OCR
3. D: attention line
4. F: ZIP code
5. G: automation
6. A: United States Postal Service
7. O: machineable mail
8. J: delivery line
9. H: ZIP+4
10. C: return address
11. I: postage stamp
12. N: BCS
13. E: destination address
14. B: address abbreviations
15. M: readable mail

Communicating Using Technology

Chapter Purpose

Chapter 8 of *Effective Communication Skills* introduces students to the use of fax machines and e-mail in communicating. Students will learn about both the advantages and disadvantages of these types of communication.

For Your Information

For more information about faxing and e-mail, check your local library for books and other sources. Two books that may be helpful are *Can I Fax a Thank-You Note?* by Audrey Glassman and *Office Emails That Really Click* by Maureen Chase and Sandy Trupp.

Additional Activity: Faxing

Some students may not be familiar with a fax machine. Find a fax machine and demonstrate how it is used.

Chapter 8 Answer Key

Check It Out 8-1

Situation No. 1

<table>
<tr><td>

To: Max Woods
Organization: The Toy Factory
Telephone No.: (213) 789-2300
Fax Number: (213) 789-2301
Date: April 27, 2002
Subject: April 1 Order

</td><td>

From: Nita Morris

Telephone No.: (424) 233-3743
Fax Number: (424) 233-3742
Number of Pages including cover: 6

</td></tr>
<tr><td colspan="2">

Message: Please check whether this order has been sent. Contact me immediately.

</td></tr>
</table>

Situation No. 2

To: *Wally's Super Sub*	**From:** *Sierra Martin*
Organization:	
Telephone No.: *(913) 557-2381*	**Telephone No.:** *(913) 557-4143*
Fax Number: *(913) 557-2382*	**Fax Number:** *(913) 557-4142*
Date: *Oct. 14, 2002*	**Number of Pages including cover:** *2*
Subject: *Lunch Order*	
Message: *Will pick up order at noon.*	

Situation No. 3

To: *Guy Simmons*	**From:** *Marty Roth*
Organization: *Simmons Realty Co.*	
Telephone No.: *(703) 576-1232*	**Telephone No.:** *(602) 814-6534*
Fax Number: *(703) 576-1231*	**Fax Number:** *(602) 814-6535*
Date: *Feb. 18, 2002*	**Number of Pages including cover:** *5*
Subject: *House at 2804 Sea Breeze Lane in Tampa, Florida*	
Message: *I am making an offer to buy this house.*	

Situation No. 4

To: *Gloria Hiatt*	**From:** *Morgan Miles*
Organization: *Southern Resorts*	
Telephone No.: *(456) 657-8901*	**Telephone No.:** *(456) 908-6790*
Fax Number: *(456) 657-8900*	**Fax Number:** *(456) 908-6789*
Date: *Sept. 28, 2002*	**Number of Pages including cover:** *3*
Subject: *Travel plans*	
Message: *Here is my travel schedule for next week.*	

Check It Out 8-2

1. Possible answers include

   E-mail is fast.
   E-mail helps people save time.
   E-mail is convenient. It doesn't need stamps or a mailbox to be sent.
   E-mail can be sent any time of day to anywhere without bothering with the time zones.
   E-mail can be saved to refer to later.
   E-mail is not limited by distance.
   E-mail is a short way to communicate in the business world.
   E-mail is almost like having a conversation.

2. Possible answers include

    When the issue is emotional
    When the issue needs to be handled immediately
    When negotiating is needed
    When a personal topic is being discussed
    When privacy is needed
    When a long list of questions needs to be answered
    When a large group of people needs to communicate about a topic

3. The subject line helps the receiver know what the e-mail contains. It helps people who get lots of e-mail to know whether it is an urgent message that needs to be handled right away.

4. E-mail address of the user; e-mail address of the receiver; brief description of the message; date, day, and time.

5. The cc (carbon copy) and Bcc (blind carbon copy) are used to send the same e-mail to others without rewriting the message.

6. To send an e-mail from one friend to another friend, you would use forwarding.

7. You may have used the wrong e-mail address. Check to see if you have the right e-mail address. Check to see if you typed the e-mail address correctly.

8. The person receiving an e-mail should have all the information needed in that e-mail. It should not be necessary to look up a previous e-mail to understand the current message.

9. The signature line indicates that the e-mail is complete. Some people don't use their name in their e-mail address. The signature helps the receiver know who has sent the e-mail.

10. Person's first name, person's full name, person's title, e-mail address, telephone number.

Check Your Vocabulary

1. A: address book	9. N: Bcc
2. O: forward	10. C: fax machine
3. E: "bounce"	11. J: e-mail address
4. L: attachment	12. M: fax number
5. D: header	13. K: body
6. B: cc	14. F: e-mail
7. G: signature	15. I: subject line
8. H: fax cover sheet	

Worksheet: Punctuation Counts

Many people use e-mail in the same way they use the telephone. E-mail is very conversational. Often e-mail messages are very hurriedly put together, are not proofread, and lack punctuation. The purpose of this activity is to help students understand the need for punctuation in e-mails and to practice using it.

Worksheet Answer Key

E-mail #1

To: Joe Wheeler
From: Lesley Fay
Re: Staff Meeting

Hi, Joe!

When is the staff meeting? Where are we meeting? Let me know before noon.

Thanks,

Lesley

E-mail #2

To: Jackie
From: Alexis
Re: Saturday Party

Hey, Jackie!

I need extra chairs for the party tonight. Do you have any? How many? Please help me. I am desperate.

Thank you,

Alexis

E-mail #3

To: Mr. Gordon Moore
From: Dr. Wendall Walters
Re: Class Opening

Dear Sir:

I regret to inform you that Geography 203 is currently a full class. However, I will place your name on a waiting list. If you do not want your name on the list, please inform me.

With regards,

Dr. Walters

E-mail #4

To: Howard Hancock
From: Natalie Cook
Re: Sales Meeting

Dear Howard,

Our sales meeting will be held in conference room 12 on Tuesday, August 17, at 3:30 p.m.

See you there,

Natalie

E-mail #5

To: Casey
From: Taylor
Re: Flight

Hi!

Meet me at the airport at 8:33 a.m. this Thursday. Can you bring Kevin with you? Can we eat breakfast at the Flapjack Palace? That would be a real treat.

See you Thursday.

Your buddy,

Taylor

E-mail #6

To: Melissa Barker
From: Helen Towns
Re: Golf Plans

Hello, Missy!

Can you play golf next Friday? I have the day off. I can meet you at 8 in the morning. Please let me know by Thursday.

Sincerely,

Helen

E-mail #7

To: Mr. James King
From: Shelley Goings
Re: Insurance Claim

Dear Mr. King:

I did not receive the correct claim form from your office. Please send the form I need as soon as possible.

Thank you,

Shelley Goings

E-mail #8

To: Roger
From: Dale
Re: Fishing

Hey, Roger!

I just got a new fishing pole. Why don't you and I go up to Loon Lake next Saturday? Bring the worms. I will bring my pole. What time shall we leave?

Your fishing pal,

Dale

E-mail #9

To: Dr. Lauren Miles
From: Dr. Charles Stine
Re: Medical Conference Rescheduling

Dear Dr. Miles:

The October 7 medical conference has been rescheduled. It will be held March 22, 2003. This decision was made at the May committee meeting.

With regards,

Dr. Charles Stine

E-mail #10

To: Ms. Sheila Foreman
From: Karlyn Carson
Re: Parent Conference

Dear Ms. Foreman,

I would like to schedule a parent conference after school next week. I am available Monday, Tuesday, and Wednesday mornings. I can come on Thursday or Friday afternoons. Please reply as soon as possible.

Sincerely,

Karlyn Carson

Punctuation Counts

Directions: The following e-mails have been written without using any punctuation. Read each e-mail. Fill in the missing punctuation.

E-mail #1

To: Joe Wheeler
From: Lesley Fay
Re: Staff Meeting

Hi Joe

When is the staff meeting   Where are we meeting   Let me know before noon

Thanks

Lesley

E-mail #2

To: Jackie
From: Alexis
Re: Saturday Party

Hey Jackie

I need extra chairs for the party tonight   Do you have any   How many   Please help me   I am desperate

Thank you

Alexis

E-mail #3

To: Mr. Gordon Moore
From: Dr. Wendall Walters
Re: Class Opening

Dear Sir

I regret to inform you that Geography 203 is currently a full class   However   I will place your name on a waiting list   If you do not want your name on the list please inform me

With regards

Dr Walters

E-mail #4

To: Howard Hancock
From: Natalie Cook
Re: Sales Meeting

Dear Howard

Our sales meeting will be held in conference room 12 on Tuesday   August 17   at 3 30 p m

See you there

Natalie

E-mail #5

To: Casey
From: Taylor
Re: Flight

Hi

Meet me at the airport at 8 33 a m this Thursday   Can you bring Kevin with you   Can we eat breakfast at the Flapjack Palace   That would be a real treat

See you Thursday

Your buddy

Taylor

E-mail #6

To: Melissa Barker
From: Helen Towns
Re: Golf Plans

Hello Missy

Can you play golf next Friday   I have the day off   I can meet you at 8 in the morning   Please let me know by Thursday

Sincerely

Helen

E-mail #7

To: Mr James King
From: Shelley Goings
Re: Insurance Claim

Dear Mr King

I did not receive the correct claim form from your office   Please send the form I need as soon as possible

Thank you

Shelley Goings

E-mail #8

To: Roger
From: Dale
Re: Fishing

Hey Roger

I just got a new fishing pole   Why don't you and I go up to Loon Lake next Saturday   Bring the worms   I will bring my pole   What time shall we leave

Your fishing pal

Dale

E-mail #9

To: Dr Lauren Miles
From: Dr Charles Stine
Re: Medical Conference Rescheduling

Dear Dr Miles

The October 7 medical conference has been rescheduled   It will be held March 22 2003   This decision was made at the May committee meeting

With regards

Dr   Charles Stine

E-mail #10

To: Ms   Sheila Foreman
From: Karlyn Carson
Re: Parent Conference

Dear Ms   Foreman

I would like to schedule a parent conference after school next week   I am available Monday   Tuesday and Wednesday mornings   I can come on Thursday or Friday afternoons   Please reply as soon as possible

Sincerely

Karlyn Carson